Note From Author:

Greetings Reader,

I am so happy that you have this book in your life. This book was created to inspire and empower you to embrace your greatness and to never forget how awesome you are.

I hope that if you ever feel sad, anxious or discouraged, you will read this book and remember to create your own happiness. This book is a simple tool to remind you that a positive way of thinking will help you lead a positive life.

Recite the affirmations on these pages daily and create your own words of encouragement for yourself and others.

Don't forget to step into your power, know your worth and be proud of who you are!

xoxo,
Kimaada

P.S. The coolest girls stand up for each other other.

DIFFERENT IS BEAUTIFUL!

I LOVE WHO I AM!
I AM PASSIONATE.

STEP INTO YOUR POWER!

I LOVE WHO I AM!
I AM CARING.

CREATE YOUR OWN SUNSHINE!

I LOVE WHO I AM!

I AM OUTGOING.

YOUR DREAM DOES NOT HAVE AN EXPIRATION DATE!

CELEBRATE EVERY TINY VICTORY!

POSITIVITY IS A SUPERPOWER!

I LOVE WHO I AM!

I AM BOLD.

SPREAD KINDNESS!

I LOVE WHO I AM!

I AM BRAVE.

BIG THINGS OFTEN HAVE SMALL BEGINNINGS!!

REAL QUEENS FIX EACH OTHERS CROWNS!

MAKE YOUR OWN MAGIC!

THERE IS ALWAYS SOMETHING TO BE THANKFUL FOR.

EVERY DAY IS
WHAT YOU MAKE IT.

MISTAKES ARE PROOF THAT YOU ARE TRYING.

YOU ARE AMAZING JUST THE WAY YOU ARE.

DO THE RIGHT THING EVEN IF NO ONE IS WATCHING.

CREATE YOUR OWN AFFIRMATIONS

CREATE YOUR OWN AFFIRMATIONS

CREATE YOUR OWN AFFIRMATIONS

CREATE YOUR OWN AFFIRMATIONS

DAILY MANTRAS

A mantra is a statement
that is repeated frequently.

Below find some daily mantras
that you can repeat to inspire you
to step into your power and
love the skin you are in.

Stand in front of a mirror,
close your eyes,
take a deep breath in a
nd look at your beautiful reflection
when saying the words.

DAILY MANTRAS

1. I am powerful and capable.

2. My mind is both curious and joyful.

3. I choose to feel good in every moment.

4. I am radiating positive vibes.

5. My mind and body are calm.

6. I am courageous.

7. My breathe is calm and slow.

8. I have a bright future.

CREATE YOUR OWN MANTRAS

CREATE YOUR OWN MANTRAS

CREATE YOUR OWN MANTRAS

CREATE YOUR OWN MANTRAS

NATUREBELLA'S KIDS BOOKS

EMPOWERMENT SERIES

I LOVE WHO I AM!
A BOOK OF AFFIRMATIONS FOR GIRLS
BY KIMAADA LE GENDRE

I LOVE WHO I AM!
GRATITUDE JOURNAL FOR GIRLS

I LOVE WHO I AM!
REFLECTIVE PRAYER JOURNAL FOR GIRLS

I LOVE WHO I AM!
MANIFESTATION PLANNER FOR GIRLS

Please check out our other Naturebella's Kids Books Series!

www.naturebellaskids.com

Lightning Source UK Ltd.
Milton Keynes UK
UKHW051257051021
391677UK00002B/145